Popular Canadian Curriculum Series

Canadian Curriculum
FrenchSmart®

Grade **4**

ISBN: 978-1-927042-16-8

Credits

Photos (Front Cover "children" Anatoliy Samara/123RF.com, "Chateau Frontenac" Susan Peterson/123RF.com
Back Cover "children" Dmitriy Shironosov/123RF.com, "classroom" Franck Boston/123RF.com, "children" Anatoliy Samara/123RF.com, "school bus" Thomas Bedenk/123RF.com)

Printed in China

Canadian Curriculum FrenchSmart

ISBN: 978-1-927042-16-8

Contents

ISBN: 978-1-927042-16-8

Les objets de classe

School Supplies

Vocabulary: Words for school supplies

Expressions: « C'est un/une... » "It's a..."
« Ce sont... » "They are..."

Grammar: Plural endings in French

un crayon
euhn kreh·yohn
a pencil

A. Copiez les mots et écrivez « m » dans la boîte si le nom est masculin et « f » s'il est féminin.

Copy the words and indicate whether they are masculine or feminine by writing either "m" or "f".

des crayons
deh kreh·yohn
some pencils

1. **un marqueur**
   euhn mar·kuhr
   a marker

In French, nouns are either masculine (m.) or feminine (f.). The article that introduces the noun tells its gender.

noun	introduced by
masculine	**un** or **le**
feminine	**une** or **la**

2. **un cahier**
   euhn kah·yeh
   a workbook

3. **une chaise**
   ewn shehz
   a chair

ISBN: 978-1-927042-16-8

4. **A** un crayon de couleur
euhn kreh·yohn duh koo·luhr
a coloured pencil

B une feuille de papier
ewn fuhy duh pah·pyeh
a sheet of paper

C la colle   *lah kohl*
glue

D un stylo   *euhn stee·loh*
a pen

E un crayon   *euhn kreh·yohn*
a pencil

F une gomme   *ewn gohm*
an eraser

5.

un tableau blanc
euhn tah·bloh blaan

a whiteboard

un sac à dos
euhn sahk ah doh

a backpack

une règle
ewn rehgl

a binder

un cartable
euhn kahr·tahbl

a ruler

B. Remplissez les boîtes avec les bons mots suivants.

Fill in the boxes with the correct words below.

le tableau noir

le crayon

la chaise

le bureau

le pupitre

le livre

la règle

le tapis

1. [ ]

luh leevr
the book

2. [ ]

luh pew·peetr
the student's desk

3. [ ]

luh bew·roh
the teacher's desk

4. [ ]

lah shehz
the chair

5. [ ]

luh tah·bloh nwahr
the blackboard

6. [ ]

luh tah·pee
the carpet

C. Écrivez les mots en français. Ensuite cherchez les mots français dans la grille.

Write the words in French. Then find the French words in the word search.

carpet

pen

eraser

binder

chair

marker

backpack

workbook

ruler

paper

g	e	w	d	s	m	h	j	o	l
v	s	a	w	q	b	a	r	b	y
c	i	d	a	t	n	è	a	f	a
x	o	y	a	c	g	a	a	r	è
i	a	p	i	l	v	f	o		t
a	i	s	e	a	d	n		a	x
s	a	t	a	d	z	a	s	k	q
		g	o	m	m	e	t	m	x
		á	n	b	i	p	y	t	d
l	u	a	j	è	k	w	l	s	s
á	k	è	e	v	a	s	o	g	a
g	c	a	r	t	a	b	l	e	c
s	g	c	h	a	i	s	e	a	à
p	b		u	l	w	b	a	u	d
a	x		q	b	n	i	s	o	
p	w	a	è	a	v	y	h	n	s
i	m	a	r	q	u	e	u	r	c
e	v	c	n	è	r	l	o	d	y
r	w	c	a	h	i	e	r		
u	d	i	á	s	x	o	k		

Plural Endings in French

When changing nouns from singular to plural, use the following word endings:

- For most words, add an "-s" to the end.
  e.g. un livre → des livre**s**

- Words that end in "-s" stay the same.
  e.g. un autobus → des autobus

- For words ending in "-eau" and "-ou", add an "-x".
  e.g. un bureau → des bureau**x**

Remember, the articles change too!

singular		plural
un/une	→	des *deh*
le/la	→	les *leh*

D. Écrivez les mots au pluriel.
Write the words in plural.

singulier singular	**pluriel** plural
le crayon	_____
le livre	_____
le pupitre	_____
un bureau	_____
une règle	_____
un tableau	_____
la chaise	_____
un stylo	_____

Expressions

C'est un crayon!

En anglais :	En français :
In English	**In French**
"It's a..."	« C'est un/une... » *seht euhn/ewn*
"They are..."	« Ce sont des... » *suh sohn deh*

E. Écrivez les expressions au singulier et au pluriel.

Write the expressions in singular and in plural.

1.

   a. C'est un _____ .

   b. Ce sont des _____ .

2.

   a. _____

   b. _____

3.

   a. _____

   b. _____

4.

   a. _____

   b. _____

Vocabulary: Words for common people and places at school

Expressions: « Est-ce que je peux aller à…? »
"May I go to…?"

Est-ce que je peux aller aux toilettes?
ehs kuh juh puh ah·leh oh twah·leht
May I go to the washroom?

A. Copiez les mots.
Copy the words.

Les endroits à l'école
Places at School

le corridor
the hallway

_____

luh ko·ree·dohr

la cour d'école
the schoolyard

_____

lah koor deh·kohl

le gymnase
the gymnasium

_____

luh jeem·nahz

la cafétéria
the cafeteria

_____

luh kah·feh·teh·ryah

la fontaine
the drinking fountain

_____

lah fohn·tehn

la classe de musique
the music class

_____

lah klass duh mew·zeek

la salle des professeurs
the teachers' lounge

_____

lah sahl deh proh·feh·suhr

la salle de classe
the classroom

_____

lah sahl duh klahs

les toilettes des filles
the girls' washroom

_____

leh twah·leht deh feey

les toilettes des garçons
the boys' washroom

_____

leh twah·leht deh gar·sohn

Ce sont les toilettes des filles!

la bibliothèque
the library

_____

lah bee·blyoh·tehk

le bureau
the office

_____

luh bew·roh

le directeur
the principal (man)

la directrice
the principal (woman)

luh dee·rehk·tuhr

lah dee·rehk·treess

un étudiant
a boy student

une étudiante
a girl student

euhn eh·tew·dyaan

ewn eh·tew·dyaant

un cahier

Library

A **le professeur** the teacher

luh proh·feh·suhr

B **la secrétaire** the secretary

luh suh·kreh·tehr

C **la bibliothécaire** the librarian

lah bee·blyoh·teh·kehr

la professeure
the teacher (woman)

le secrétaire
the secretary (man)

le bibliothécaire
the librarian (man)

la concierge
the caretaker (woman)

D **le concierge** the caretaker

luh kohn·syehrj

ISBN: 978-1-927042-16-8

B. Dessinez le bon sexe. Identifiez chaque personne dans l'image.

Draw the correct gender. Identify each person in the picture.

○ le concierge ○ l'étudiant

○ le professeur ○ la secrétaire ○ la directrice

1.

2.

3.

4.

5.

C. **Mettez chaque activité (A-C) dans le bon endroit. Ensuite écrivez le nom de chaque endroit.**

Put each activity (A-C) in the correct place. Then write the name of the place.

la cafétéria   la salle de classe
la cour d'école

1.

2.

3.

Expressions

Est-ce que je peux aller à la cour d'école?
ehs kuh juh puh ah·leh ah lah koor deh·kohl

En anglais :
In English

"May I go to...?"

En français :
In French

« Est-ce que je peux aller à...? »

ehs kuh juh puh ah·leh ah

D. Complétez les questions à l'aide des images et des mots donnés.

Complete the questions with the help of the pictures and the given words.

1.

Est-ce que je peux aller à

_____ ?

the music class

2.

Est-ce que je peux aller à

_____ ?

the library

3.

_____

_____

the classroom

Vocabulary: Family members

Expressions: « Voici... »
"Here is..."

Grammar: Expressing possession
with "de"

Voici l'animal domestique de la famille!
vwah·see lah·nee·mahl doh·mehs·teek
duh lah fah·meey
Here is the family pet!

A. Copiez les mots.
Copy the words.

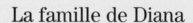

La famille de Diana
lah fah·meey duh dyah·nah
Diana's family

la mère
lah mehr

_____

le père
luh pehr

_____

la sœur
lah seuhr

_____

le frère
luh frehr

_____

le bébé
luh beh·beh

_____

mother

father

sister

brother

baby

Diana

l'animal
domestique

pet

*lah·nee·mahl
doh·mehs·teek*

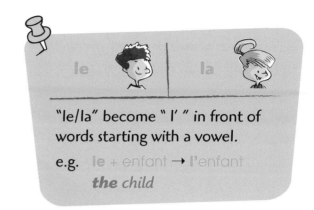

le | la

"le/la" become " l' " in front of
words starting with a vowel.

e.g. le + enfant → l'enfant
the child

le cousin

cousin (boy)

luh koo·zahn

la cousine

cousin (girl)

lah koo·zeen

le grand-père
grandfather

_____

luh graan·pehr

l'oncle
uncle

_____

lohnkl

le fils
son

_____

luh feess

la grand-mère
grandmother

_____

lah graan·mehr

la tante
aunt

_____

lah taant

la fille
daughter

_____

lah feey

ISBN: 978-1-927042-16-8 **Canadian Curriculum FrenchSmart** · Grade 4   17

B. Remplissez les tirets pour identifier les membres de la famille.
Fill in the blanks to identify the members of the family.

- gra__ __-p__ __e

- gr__n__-mè__ __

- f__ __le

- f__ __s

- a__ima__ d__m__sti__ue

- m__r__

- p__ __e

- f__ __re

- b__b__

- __œ__r

C. **Créez votre arbre généalogique.**
Create your family tree.

Mon arbe généalogique

Expressions

En anglais :	En français :
In English	In French
"Here is…"	« Voici… »
	vwah·see

Voici mon frère!
vwah·see mohn frehr
Here is my brother!

D. **Remplissez les tirets et trouvez le mot mystère.**
Fill in the blanks and find the mystery word.

Voici le __ __ls

____ le gr __ nd-p__ __ __

____ la __ è__ __

____ la cous __ ne

____ la fi __ __ __

____ l'o__ __ __ e

____ le p__ __ __

l'oncle

le fils

la cousine

la fille

la mère

le grand-père

le père

Mot mystère :
Mystery word

Expressing Possession with "de"

The French preposition "de" can be used to indicate possession. It goes after the possessed object/person and before the possessor.

e.g. la sœur **de** Marcel
      the sister **of** Marcel/Marcel's sister

E. Remplissez les tirets selon l'arbre généalogique.
Fill in the blanks according to the family tree.

> **Voici Jean, le père de Marcel.**
> *vwah·see jaan luh pehr duh mahr·sehl*
> Here is Jean, Marcel's father.

1. Voici Christie, ___ _____ de Marcel.

2. Voici Susanne, ___ _____ - _____ de Pierre.

3. Voici Marie, ___ _____ de Claire.

4. Voici _____ , l'oncle ___ Marie.

5. Voici Marcel, ___ _____ de Claire.

Les jours de la semaine

The Days of the Week

Vocabulary: Days of the week

Expressions: « Je vais à... » "I go to..."

> **Le lundi, je vais à l'école!**
> *luh luhn·dee juh veh zah leh·kohl*
> *On Monday, I go to school!*

A. Copiez les mots.

Copy the words.

lundi
luhn·dee

_____
Monday

mardi
mahr·dee

_____
Tuesday

mercredi
mehr·cruh·dee

_____
Wednesday

jeudi
juh·dee

_____
Thursday

vendredi
vaan·druh·dee

_____
Friday

samedi
sahm·dee

_____
Saturday

dimanche
dee·maansh

_____
Sunday

les jours de la semaine
leh joor duh lah suh·mehn

_____

the days of the week

la date
lah daht

_____

the date

une semaine
ewn suh·mehn

_____

a week

un jour
euhn joor

_____

a day

le calendrier
luh kah·laan·dree·yeh

_____

the calendar

B. Numérotez les jours de la semaine du premier (1) au dernier (7).
Number the days of the week from first to last (1–7).

○ jeudi   ○ lundi

○ dimanche   ○ samedi

○ mercredi   ○ mardi   ○ vendredi

In French, the week starts with Monday, not Sunday.

Attention!

In French, the days of the week start with a lower case letter while in English, they start with a capital letter.

e.g.
mercredi
Wednesday

C. **Remplissez les tirets avec les bonnes lettres.**
Fill in the blanks with the correct letters.

les jo__ __s de la s__ __ai__ __

- l__ __d__

- m__ __di

- m__r__ __ed__

- j__ __d__

- __e__dr__ __ __ __

- s__ __ __di

- __i__an__ __ __

le
c__ __en__r__ __ __ __

un
j__ __ __ __

ISBN: 978-1-927042-16-8

D. Copiez les mots. Mettez les jours de la semaine dans le bon ordre.

Copy the words. Put the days of the week in the correct order.

The French say both "la fin de semaine" and "le week-end"!

les jours de la semaine ■weekdays
leh joor duh lah suh·mehn

les j_____

la fin de semaine ■ the weekend
lah fahn duh suh·mehn

la f_____

E. **Utilisez la clé pour trouver les mots mystères.**
Use the key to find the mystery words.

la clé
lah kleh

_____

the key

A ∿ B ⌓ C ▯ D ◯ E ⊙ F ⌈ G ▢

H ⚇ I ⦨ J A K ⦙ L ⌒○ M ⧺ N ⌒○○ O ≈ P ⟋⟍

Q ♀ R ⛛ S ⨯ T ⊖ U ⊹ V ⌄ W ⌇ X △ Y ◗ Z ⌇

1. A ⊙ ⊹ ◯ ⦨

    _____

2. ⨯ ∿ ⧺ ⊙ ◯ ⦨

    _____

3. ⌄ ⊙ ⌒○○ ◯ ⛛ ⊙ ◯ ⦨

    _____

4. ▯ ∿ ⌒○ ⊙ ⌒○○ ◯ ⛛ ⦨ ⊙ ⛛

    _____

5. ⌒○ ∿ ⌈ ⦨ ⌒○○ ◯ ⊙ ⨯ ⊙ ⧺ ∿ ⦨ ⌒○○ ⊙

    _____

ISBN: 978-1-927042-16-8

Expressions

Je vais à la salle des professeurs.
juh veh zah lah sahl deh proh·feh·suhr

I am going to the teachers' lounge.

En anglais :	**En français :**
In English	**In French**
"I go/am going to…"	« Je vais à… » *juh veh zah*

F. Remplissez les tirets avec les jours de la semaine et l'expression « je vais à... ».

Fill in the blanks with the days of the week and the expression "I go to…".

1. Le _____ , _____ la bibliothèque.
   Monday

2. Le _____ , _____ la salle de classe.
   Tuesday

3. Le _____ , _____ la classe de musique.
   Wednesday

4. Le _____ , _____ la cour d'école.
   Thursday

5. Le _____ ,
   Friday

   _____ l'école.

6. Le _____ ,
   Saturday

   _____ la fontaine.

7. Le _____ ,
   Sunday

   _____ la pêche.

la pêche
lah pehsh

_____
fishing

Unité 5
Les mois de l'année
The Months of the Year

Vocabulary: Months of the year

Expressions: « Aujourd'hui c'est... » "Today is..."

> **Aujourd'hui c'est le 14 février!**
>
> *oh·joor·dwee seh luh kah·tohrz feh·vree·yeh*
>
> *Today is February 14th!*

A.   Copiez les mots.
Copy the words.

Les mois de l'année
the months of the year

_____

leh mwah duh ahnay

décembre
December

_____

deh·saambr

janvier
January

_____

jaan·vyeh

février
February

_____

feh·vree·yeh

mars
March

_____

mahrs

avril
April

_____

ah·vreel

mai
May

_____

meh

juin
June

_____

jew·ahn

juillet
July

_____

jwee·yeh

août
August

_____

oot

septembre
September

_____

sehp·taambr

octobre
October

_____

ohk·tohbr

novembre
November

_____

noh·vaambr

B. Écrivez le nom de votre mois favori.
Write the name of your favourite month.

mon mois préféré :
my favourite month

Attention!

In English, the names of the months begin with a capital letter but in French, they begin with a lower case letter unless they are at the beginning of the sentence.

C. Écrivez le mois correspondant sous chaque image.

Write the corresponding month under each picture.

mai   janvier   août   octobre

1.

2.

3.

4.

D. Remplissez les tirets pour compléter le nom du mois.

Fill in the blanks to complete the name of the month.

 __a__vi__ __

 __év__ __ __ __ __

__ __rs

 __v__ __l

 __a__

 __u__ __

__ __il__ __ __

 __oû__

 __ __pt__ __b__ __ __

 __c__o__ __ __

 __ __ve__ __r__

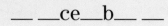 __ __ce__b__ __

ISBN: 978-1-927042-16-8 **Canadian Curriculum FrenchSmart** · Grade 4

E. **Trouvez les mois cachés dans la grille et écrivez-les dans le bon ordre.**
Find the names of the months in the word search and write them in the correct order.

r	s	d	e	f	h	k	z	d	p	m	a	r	s
s	v	s	d	é	c	e	m	b	r	e			e
e	j	a	n	v	i	e	r	c	j				p
i	u			r	d	i	s	l	u				t
a	i			i	s	c	m	a	i				e
v	l			e	m	d	o	p	n				m
r	l			r	x	s	w	h	f				b
i	e			n	n	o	v	e	m	b	r	e	r
l	t	m	a	o	û	t	o	c	t	o	b	r	e

_____

_____

_____   _____

_____   _____

_____   _____

_____   _____

Les mois de l'année

Saying the Date

En anglais :
In English

Today is **day** , **month**
date , 2013.

En français :
In French

Aujourd'hui c'est le **day** **date**
month 2013.

oh·joor·dwee seh luh...duh·meel·trehz

Aujourd'hui c'est le mercredi 24 avril 2013.
oh·joor·dwee seh luh mehr·cruh·dee vahnt·kahtr ah·vreel duh·meel·trehz

Today is Wednesday, April 24ᵗʰ, 2013.

F. Écrivez la date.
Write the date.

1. **A** Aujourd'hui c'est le

   _____ _____ 2013.

   B _____

   _____

   C _____

   _____

2. Write today's date.

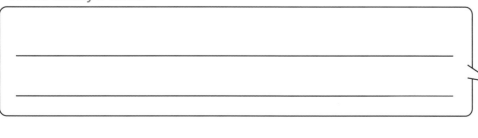

ISBN: 978-1-927042-16-8

Les nombres : de 1 à 15

Numbers: 1 to 15

Il y a quinze ballons.
eel ee yah kahnz bah·lohn
There are fifteen balls.

Vocabulary: Numbers 1 to 15

Expressions: « Il y a... »
"There is/are..."

cinq

deux

un

quatre

huit

treize

douze

sept

trois

six

neuf

onze

quinze

dix

quatorze

A. Copiez les mots.

Copy the words.

les nombres the numbers _____

leh nohmbr

un one

deux two

trois three

_____

_____

_____

euhn

duh

trwah

quatre four

cinq five

six six

_____

_____

_____

kahtr

sahnk

seess

ISBN: 978-1-927042-16-8

sept seven

_____

seht

huit eight

_____

weet

neuf nine

_____

nuhf

dix ten

_____

deess

onze eleven

_____

ohnz

douze twelve

_____

dooz

treize thirteen

_____

trehz

quatorze fourteen

_____

kah·tohrz

quinze fifteen

_____

kahnz

B. Coloriez le nombre d'objets indiqué.
Colour the number of objects indicated.

1. cinq

2. neuf

3. deux

4. sept

C. Comptez les objets. Ensuite encerclez la bonne réponse.

Count the objects. Then circle the correct answer.

1.

quatre

cinq

treize

quinze

2.

douze

huit

3.

onze

dix

4.

trois

sept

5.

quatorze

douze

D. Comptez les objets. Écrivez les nombres.
Count the objects. Write the numbers.

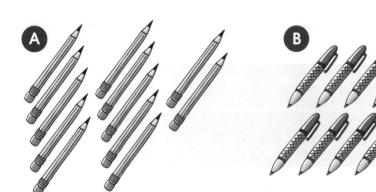

A

B

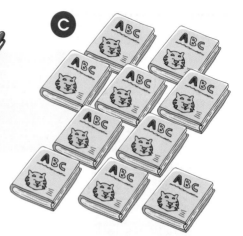

C

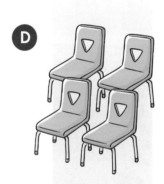

La liste d'achats
The Shopping List

A _____ cr__y__ __s

B _____ s__yl__ __

C _____ ca__ __ __ __s

D _____ c__ __is__ __

E _____ paires de

c__ __e__ __ __

D

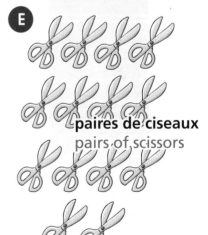

E

paires de ciseaux
pairs of scissors

E.   **Lisez la recette de salade de fruits. Écrivez les nombres en lettres.**
Read the recipe for a fruit salad. Write the numbers in words.

les pommes
leh pohm

les fraises
leh frehz

les grains de raisin
leh grahn duh reh·zahn

les bananes
leh bah·nahn

le melon d'eau
luh muh·lohn doh

les tasses
de jus d'orange
leh tahs duh jew doh·rannj

 coupez
koo·peh
cut

 ajoutez
ah·joo·teh
add

 mesurez
muh·zu·reh
measure

La salade de fruits
Fruit Salad

 5   Coupez   c___ __ __   p__ __ __ __ __ __ .

 12   Ajoutez _____ _____ .

 4   C_____ _____ _____ .

 15   A_____ _____ _____ .

 1   C_____ _____ _____ .

 8   Mesurez _____ tasses de jus _____ .

ISBN: 978-1-927042-16-8

 **Expressions**

En anglais :	**En français :**
In English	In French
"There is/are..."	« Il y a... »
	eel ee yah

> **Il y a trois oiseaux!**
> *eel ee yah trwah zwah·zoh*
> *There are three birds!*

F. Complétez les phrases avec l'expression « Il y a... ».

Complete the sentences with the expression "Il y a...".

1.

   _____ deux crayons.

2.

   _____ _____ règles.

3.

   _____ _____ stylos.

4.

   _____ _____ cartables.

5.

   _____ _____ marqueurs.

Unité 7

L'heure et le temps du jour

The Hour and the Time of Day

Vocabulary: Words related to time

Expressions: « Quelle heure est-il? »
"What time is it?"

« Il est... »
"It is..."

> **Quelle heure est-il?**
> kehl uhr eh·teel
> What time is it?

> **Il est 11 h 30.**
> eel eh ohnz uhr traant
> It is eleven thirty.

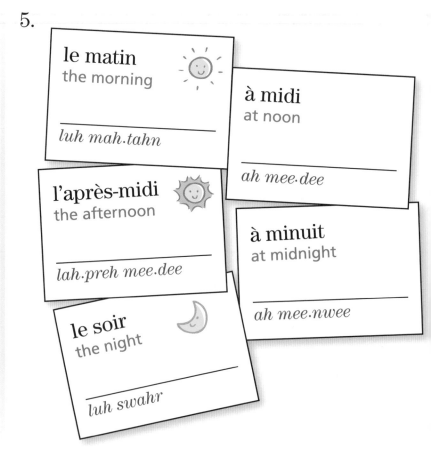

A. Copiez les mots.
Copy the words.

1. l'heure   the time

_____
luhr

2. une horloge   a clock

_____
ewn ohr·lohj

3. une heure   an hour

_____
ewn uhr

4. une minute   a minute

_____
ewn mee·newt

5.

le matin
the morning
_____
luh mah·tahn

à midi
at noon
_____
ah mee·dee

l'après-midi
the afternoon
_____
lah·preh mee·dee

à minuit
at midnight
_____
ah mee·nwee

le soir
the night
_____
luh swahr

Writing the Time

En anglais : In English	En français : In French
3:00	3 h
8:15	8 h 15
5:30	5 h 30

B. **Écrivez l'heure en français.**

Write the time in French.

1.

_____

2.

_____

3.

_____

4.

5. 2:44 _____

6. 7:30 _____

7. 8:00 _____

8. 12:26 _____

In French, we tell the time using a 24-hour clock. Instead of starting over at 1 after noon (12:00 p.m.), the 24-hour clock continues to count: 13, 14, 15, etc. So when you go to bed at 10 p.m., it's really 22 h.

11:30 p.m.

23 h 30

Remember, the minutes stay the same!

C. **Utilisez l'horloge de 24 heures pour écrire l'heure en français.**

Use the 24-hour clock to write the time in French.

1. 4:25 a.m. 2. 6:37 p.m. 3. 5:11 p.m.

_____   _____   _____

4. 7:03 a.m. 5. 10:20 p.m. 6.

_____   _____

7. 1:05 a.m. 8. 1:45 p.m.

_____   _____

D. Remplissez les tirets. Écrivez l'expression temporelle qui correspond à l'heure donnée.

Fill in the blanks. Write the time of the day that matches the given time.

Le temps du jour
The time of day

le m__ __in

l'a__ __ès-m__ __i

le s__ __r

1. 23 h 15 _____

2. 8 h 30 _____

3. 15 h 26 _____

4. 22 h 40 _____

5. 14 h 13 _____

6. 20 h 04 _____

7.

8 h 45

_____

E. **Encerclez l'heure correspondante à l'image. Écrivez l'expression temporelle qui correspond à l'heure.**

Circle the time shown in the picture. Write the time of the day that matches the time.

1.

14 h 30

8 h 10   18 h 45

_____

2.

20 h 14

9 h 30   11 h 05

_____

3.

4 h 15

21 h 30   16 h

_____

Asking the Time

En anglais :	En français :
In English	**In French**
Question: "What time is it?"	Question : « Quelle heure est-il? »
Answer: "It is..."	*kehl uhr eh·teel*
	Réponse : « Il est... »
	eel eh

Quelle heure est-il?

Il est 13 h.

F. Remplissez les tirets. Répondez aux questions selon l'heure à chaque ville.

Fill in the blanks. Answer the questions according to the time in each city.

Paris

Toronto

Londres

A Quelle heure est-il à P_____ ?

_____

B Quelle _____ _____ à _____ ?

_____

C Quelle _____ _____ à _____ ?

_____

Les pronoms personnels sujets

Personal Subject Pronouns

Vocabulary: Personal subject pronouns

Grammar: The verb « avoir » "to have"

J'ai trois frères!
jeh trwah frehr
I have three brothers!

A. Copiez les mots.
Copy the words.

| singulier (sg.) | | pluriel (pl.) | |
| singular | | plural | |

 je I

_____
juh

 nous we

_____
noo

 tu you (sg.)

_____
tew

 vous you (pl.)

_____
voo

 il he

_____
eel

 ils they (m.)

_____
eel

 elle she

_____
ehl

 elles they (f.)

_____
ehl

ISBN: 978-1-927042-16-8

Les pronoms personnels singuliers
Singular Personal Pronouns

Il masculin
He/It masculine

- masculine singular common nouns
  e.g. le garçon

- masculine proper nouns
  e.g. Jean

→ can be replaced by **"il"**
  e.g. le garçon → **il**
        Jean → **il**

Elle féminin
She/It feminine

- feminine singular common nouns
  e.g. la fille

- feminine proper nouns
  e.g. Sarah

→ can be replaced by **"elle"**
  e.g. la fille → **elle**
        Sarah → **elle**

B. Remplacez les noms avec le pronom « il » ou « elle ».
Replace the nouns with the pronoun "il" or "elle".

1. Caroline
   le chien

2. la tante _____

3. la semaine _____

4. le directeur _____

5. un sac à dos _____

6. la gomme _____

7. Simon _____

8. une chaise _____

9. le bureau _____

10. la règle _____

Les pronoms personnels pluriels
Plural Personal Pronouns

Ils masculin
They masculine

- masculine plural common nouns
  e.g. **les** garçon**s**

- more than one masculine proper noun
  e.g. Jean et Pierre

- any group of nouns with at least one masculine noun
  e.g. Marie, Julie et Jean

→ can be replaced by **"ils"**

e.g. les garçons → **ils**

  Jean et Pierre → **ils**

  Pierre, Jean et Julie → **ils**

Elles féminin
They feminine

- feminine plural common nouns
  e.g. **les** fille**s**

- more than one feminine proper noun
  e.g. Sarah et Julie

→ can be replaced by **"elles"**

e.g. les filles → **elles**

  Sarah et Marie → **elles**

C. Remplacez les noms avec le pronom « ils » ou « elles ».
Replace the nouns with the pronoun "ils" or "elles".

1. le cousin et la cousine   _____

2. Pierre, Julie et les chiennes   _____

3. Marie, Sarah et Caroline   _____

4.  **les règles (f.)**   5. les livres (m.)   _____

6. les pupitres (m.)   _____

7. les chiens   _____

_____

ISBN: 978-1-927042-16-8

AVOIR au présent
To have

singular	plural
J'**ai** *jeh* I have	Nous **avons** *noo zah·vohn* We have
Tu **as** *tew ah* You have	Vous **avez** *voo zah·veh* You (pl.) have
Il **a** *eel ah* He has	Ils **ont** *eel zohn* They (m.) have
Elle **a** *ehl ah* She has	Elles **ont** *ehl zohn* They (f.) have

> The pronoun "je" becomes "j'" before a vowel.
>
> je + ai = j'ai
>
> *I have*

D. Complétez les phrases avec la bonne forme du verbe « avoir ».

Complete the sentences with the correct form of the verb "avoir".

1. Elle _____ un crayon.

2. Nous _____ des grains de raisin.

3. Ils _____ un animal domestique.

4. Vous _____ sept marqueurs.

5. Tu _____ cinq paires de ciseaux.

6. Elles _____ deux chaises.

7.

J'_____ une boîte de jus orange.
one box of orange juice

E. Reliez chaque pronom à la bonne phrase.
Match each pronoun with the correct phrase.

Il •

Vous •

Ils •

Elle •

Nous •

Elles •

• ont des stylos.
have pens.

• a une gomme.
has an eraser.

• avons deux feuilles de papier.
have two pieces of paper.

• avez une règle.
have a ruler.

• ai des chaises.
have chairs.

• a des crayons.
has pencils.

• as des professeurs.
have teachers.

• ont des cahiers.
have workbooks.

ISBN: 978-1-927042-16-8

F. **Lisez l'histoire et encerclez les pronoms qui pourraient remplacer les mots.**

Read the story and circle the pronouns that could replace the words.

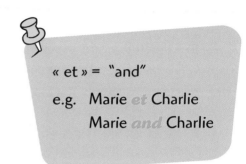

« et » = "and"

e.g. Marie *et* Charlie
      Marie *and* Charlie

1. **Ils   Nous   Vous   de**
    (Le père et la mère)

Marcel   ont   deux   filles   et   deux   fils.

2. **Vous   Je   Il**   a deux sœurs.   3. **Elle   Elles   Ils**
    (Marcel)   *(Les deux sœurs de Marcel)*

ont un animal domestique, Charlie.   4. **Tu   Vous   Il**
                                              (Marcel)

a aussi un frère, Pierre.   5. **Il   Nous   Je**   , le bébé, a une balle.
                                    (Pierre)

6. **Elles   Nous   Ils**   ont une maison.
(Marcel, les deux sœurs de Marcel, Charlie et Pierre)

Chez moi

At My House

Vocabulary: Household objects

Grammar: The verb « être » "to be"

Expressions: « Où est... ? » "Where is...?"

« Il/Elle est dans... » "It's in..."

> ***Chez moi, la baignoire est dans la chambre à coucher.***
> *sheh mwah lah behy·nwahr eh daan lah shaambr ah koo·sheh*
> *At my house, the bathtub is in the bedroom.*

A. Copiez les mots.

Copy the words.

la salle à manger
the dining room

_____

lah sahl ah maan·jeh

la chambre à coucher
the bedroom

_____

lah shaambr ah koo·sheh

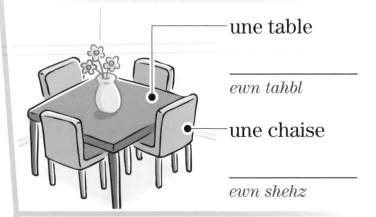

une table

_____

ewn tahbl

un oreiller

_____

euhn oh·reh·yeh

une chaise

_____

ewn shehz

la cuisine
the kitchen

_____

lah kwee·zeen

un lit

_____

euhn lee

un réfrigérateur

_____

euhn reh·free·jeh·rah·tuhr

ISBN: 978-1-927042-16-8

le salon
the living room

_____

luh sah·lohn

la buanderie
the laundry room

_____

lah bew·aan·dree

une lampe

_____

ewn laamp

une télévision

_____

ewn teh·leh·vee·zyohn

un fauteuil

_____

euhn foh·teuhy

un canapé

_____

euhn kah·nah·peh

une machine à laver

_____

ewn mah·sheen ah lah·veh

la salle de bain
the washroom

_____

lah sahl duh bahn

une baignoire

_____

ewn behy·nwahr

une toilette

_____

ewn twah·leht

la maison the house

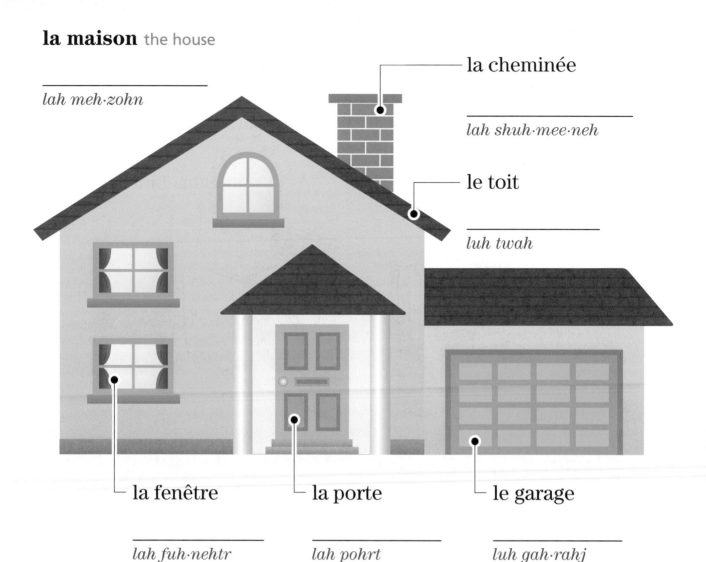

_____

lah meh·zohn

la cheminée

_____

lah shuh·mee·neh

le toit

_____

luh twah

la fenêtre

_____

lah fuh·nehtr

la porte

_____

lah pohrt

le garage

_____

luh gah·rahj

B. Encerclez les objets qui se trouvent dans chaque pièce.

Circle the objects that would be found in each room.

1. **la salle à manger**

   une table

   un oreiller

   une toilette

   une chaise

2. **le salon**

   un lit

   une lampe

   un canapé

   une baignoire

3. **la chambre à coucher**

   un oreiller

   une machine à laver

   un lit

   un réfrigérateur

ISBN: 978-1-927042-16-8

ÊTRE au présent
To be

singular	plural
Je **suis** I am *juh swee*	Nous **sommes** We are *noo sohm*
Tu **es** You are *tew eh*	Vous **êtes** You are *voo zeht*
Il **est** He is *eel eh*	Ils **sont** They (m.) are *eel sohn*
Elle **est** She is *ehl eh*	Elles **sont** They (f.) are *ehl sohn*

C. **Remplissez les tirets avec la bonne forme du verbe « être ».**

Fill in the blanks with the correct form of the verb "être".

1. Elle _____ une fille. She is a girl.
   ewn feey

2. Vous _____ fâchés. You (pl.) are angry.
   fah·sheh

3. Ils _____ fâchés. They (pl.) are angry.

4. Je _____ heureux! I am happy!
   uh·ruh

5.
   Tu _____ une fille.

   Tu _____ un garçon.

Expressions

OÙ
Where

En anglais :
In English

Question: "Where is...?"

Answer: "It is **in**..."

En français :
In French

Question : « Où est...? »
oo eh

Réponse : « Il/Elle est **dans**... »
eel/ehl eh daan

> *Où est la lampe?*
> *oo eh lah laamp*
> *Where is the lamp?*

D. **Répondez aux questions par des phrases complètes.**
Answer the questions with complete sentences.

Où est...

1. la toilette?

   Elle est dans la salle de _____ .

2. la table?

   _____

3. le canapé?

   _____

4. le réfrigérateur?

   _____

5. le lit?

   _____

6. la machine à laver?

   _____

E. Demandez l'endroit de chaque objet avec « Où est... ».

Ask the location of each object using "Où est...".

F. Écrivez la bonne réponse.

Write the correct answer.

1.

Où est la cheminée?

Elle est sur _____ .
on   *le salon/le toit*

2.

A   Où est le fauteuil?

B   Où est la baignoire?

A _____

_____

B _____

C   Où est le lit?

_____

C _____

_____

Les couleurs

Colours

Vocabulary: Words for colours

Grammar: Different forms of colour adjectives

Expressions: « J'aime... » "I like..."

« Je n'aime pas... » "I don't like..."

J'aime le rose!
jehm luh rohz
I like pink!

A.   Copiez les mots.

Copy the words.

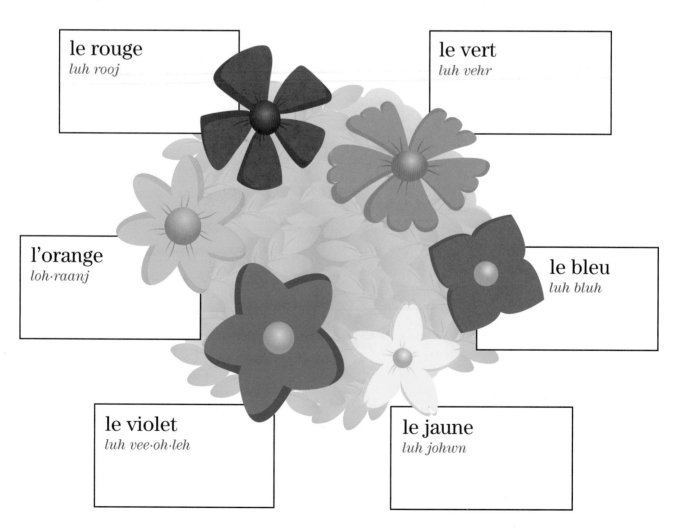

le rouge
luh rooj

le vert
luh vehr

l'orange
loh·raanj

le bleu
luh bluh

le violet
luh vee·oh·leh

le jaune
luh johwn

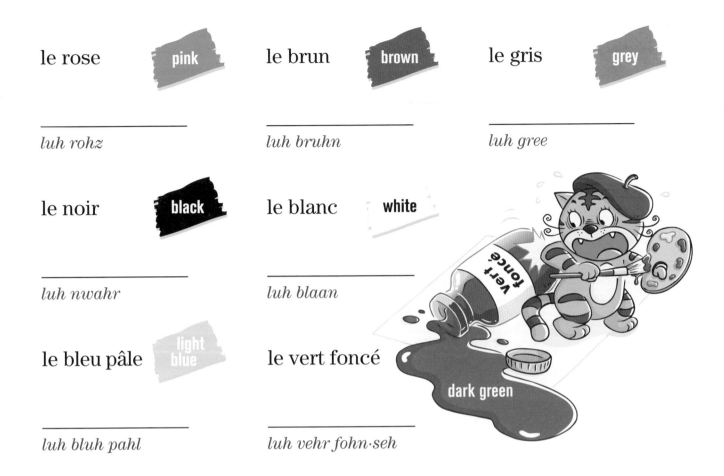

le rose — pink

luh rohz

le brun — brown

luh bruhn

le gris — grey

luh gree

le noir — black

luh nwahr

le blanc — white

luh blaan

le bleu pâle — light blue

luh bluh pahl

le vert foncé — dark green

luh vehr fohn·seh

B. Quelle couleur obtient-on lorsqu'on mélange chaque paire de couleurs?
What colour do we get by mixing each pair of colours?

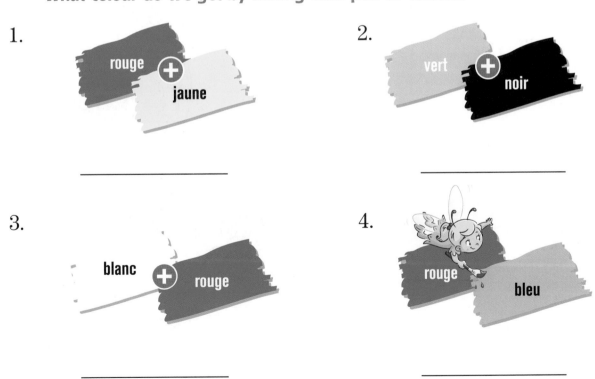

1. rouge + jaune

2. vert + noir

3. blanc + rouge

4. rouge bleu

C. **Reliez chaque mot anglais au bon mot français. Ensuite coloriez l'arc-en-ciel avec les couleurs indiquées.**

Link each English word to the correct French word. Then colour the rainbow with the indicated colours.

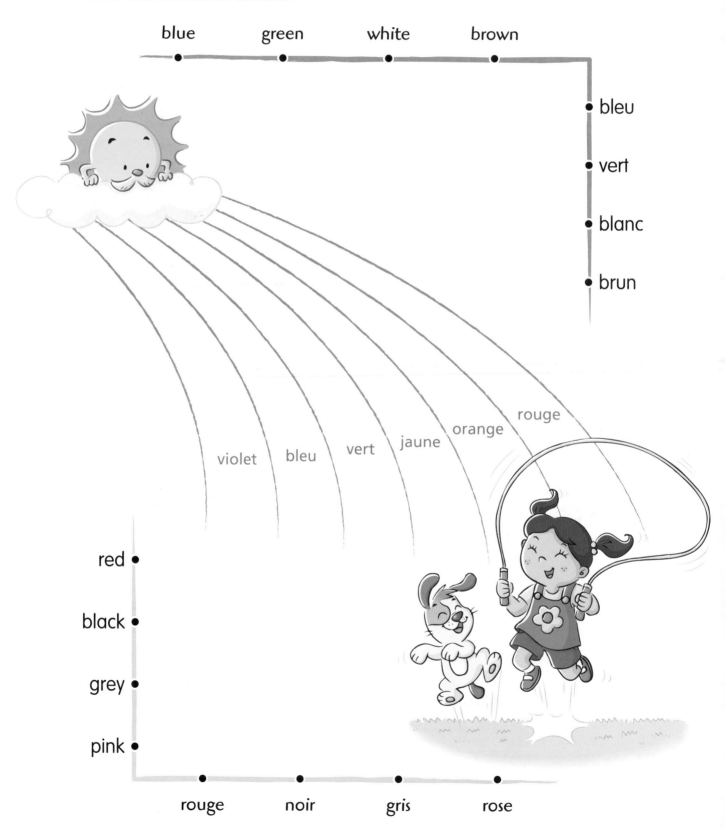

blue   green   white   brown

bleu

vert

blanc

brun

rouge

orange

jaune

vert

bleu

violet

red

black

grey

pink

rouge   noir   gris   rose

D. Écrivez la couleur de chaque objet.

Write the colour of each object.

1.

2.

3.

4.

5.

6.

7.

Colour Adjectives

French adjectives must agree in number and gender with the nouns they describe. Colour words can be used as adjectives. They are placed after the nouns they are describing.

Masculine		Feminine	
Singular	Plural	Singular	Plural
bleu	bleus	bleue	bleues
vert	verts	verte	vertes
violet	violets	violette	violettes
blanc	blancs	blanche	blanches
rouge	rouges	rouge	rouges
orange	orange	orange	orange

"Orange" and two-word colour adjectives (bleu pâle, vert foncé, etc.) are exceptions that never change form.

E. **Complétez les phrases avec la bonne forme du verbe « avoir » et la bonne forme des adjectifs de couleurs.**

Complete the sentences with the correct form of the verb "avoir" and colour adjectives.

A Vous _____ des règles _____ .

B _____

C _____

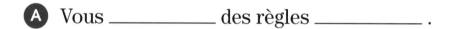

D _____

Expressions

En anglais : **In English**	**En français :** **In French**
"I like..."	« J'aime... » *jehm*
"I don't like..."	« Je n'aime pas... » *juh nehm pah*

> **J'aime le rouge!**
 jehm luh rooj
 I like red!

F. **Écrivez les expressions « J'aime... » et « Je n'aime pas... » avec les couleurs données.**

Write the expressions "J'aime..." and "Je n'aime pas..." with the given colours.

_____

_____

_____

_____

_____

_____

_____

_____

La révision

A. Encerclez la bonne réponse.
Circle the correct answer.

1.
   un livre

   un tableau

   un stylo

2.
   un bureau

   un cahier

   une paire de ciseaux

4.

   un oreiller

   une toilette

   un canapé

3.

   des frères

   des sœurs

   une tante

5.
   la cuisine

   la salle à manger

   le salon

6.
   le brun

   le blanc

   le vert

ISBN: 978-1-927042-16-8

7.

| ils | elle | nous |

8.

mardi

mercredi

?

vendredi

lundi

dimanche

jeudi

9.

4 h 40   16 h 40   14 h 40

10.

la bibliothèque

la cour d'école

la salle de classe

11.

une télévision

un réfrigérateur

une machine à laver

12.

cinq   neuf   huit

ISBN: 978-1-927042-16-8   **Canadian Curriculum FrenchSmart** · Grade 4

B. Remplissez les tirets pour écrire les noms des objets.

Fill in the blanks to write the names of the objects.

le grand-père

D octobre novembre ?

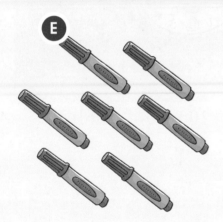

A l__ __ __ti__

B l__ __ra__ __-__ __re

C q__ __t__ __

D dé__ __ __ __ r__

E s__ __t __ar__ __ __ __ __ __ __

F l__ b__ __ __

G l__ __r__ __o__

H l__ c__ __ap__

I l__ __e__ t__ __

J l__ __am__ __

ISBN: 978-1-927042-16-8

C. Mettez les lettres dans les bons cercles.
Put the letters in the correct circles.

A J'aime...

B Elle est dans...

C Quelle heure est-il?

D Il est 16 h.

E Il

F Nous sommes...

G Tu...

H Elles sont...

I Où est...?

Simon

You...

◯ I like...   ◯ Where is...?

◯ We are...   ◯ It is in...

They are...

What time is it?   It is 4 p.m.

D. Écrivez les bonnes lettres dans les cercles.
Write the correct letters in the circles.

1. Quelle heure est-il? _____ ◯

A C'est le 24 mars.   **B** Il est 8 h 30.   **C** Il y a un bébé.

2. Il y a sept paires de ciseaux. _____ ◯

A    **B**    **C**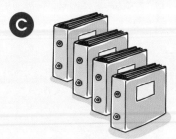

3. Est-ce que je peux aller à la cafétéria? _____ ◯

A    **B**    **C**

4. Où est le lit? _____ ◯

A 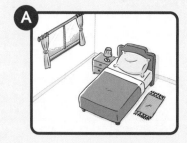   **B**    **C**

5.   Voici ma grand-mère. ——————————— ◯

A

B

C

6.   J'ai des pommes. ——————————— ◯

A

B

C

7.   Je n'aime pas le rouge. ——————————— ◯

A

B

C

8.   Ce sont des règles. ——————————— ◯

A

B

C

Faites les mots croisés.

Complete the crossword puzzle.

un chat
euhn shah

un chapeau
euhn shah·poh

la crème glacée
lah krehm glah·seh

le biscuit
luh bees·kwee

une grenouille
ewn gruh·nooy

la robe
lah rohb

Je porte un ___1___ !
juh pohrt euhn shah·poh
I am wearing a hat!

Voici une ___3___ !

Il y a un ___2___ !

Tu portes une ___2___ !
tew pohrt ewn rohb
You are wearing a dress!

J'aime le ___1___ !

Mots cachés - Word Search

Trouvez les mots cachés dans la grille.
Find the words in the word search.

```
                                    y u c a a s y
                                    o ô o k p a s
w y x i y c u v a o û t o w u v o c f
l q l l l a l i t a r b k a s g m à v
b c y ê a r a k a d t v a œ i r m d j
b a h a m t m q h d s œ u r n u e o a
p r s ô p a u j o c a i u r e â a s b
e h ê a e b h f r e p a a r v o e s l
b e u u h l k p l s h s x t v a p c v
e y g e m e c v o h r f a a s a a z j
o u b è w œ w x g c y        b a f a e s
x w x x v ô p s e            c z t v
q w c e g b g h x(           s f
f â k r k c f z r
c g x w a z a q s a
ü o ê r o y t i j k â
j a a y d h o e u p è
s ù w a c a a n a ï a
t m i h z k p â y u ç
n z n g
```

cartable

sœur

chaise

table

sac à dos

livre

règle

crayon

gomme

noir

Canadian Curriculum FrenchSmart · Grade 4

ISBN: 978-1-927042-16-8

```
m r t p a o e r x y o p a ê q v k g l d
â f z j b x c r t w u r a w w w l q m w
e c h a i s e b w q a q e a e a i t a t
é v z t a s o g d r f x r i a s v d a y
h t u v a b j o r è r o é f l k r i c x
ô b a r a b a m j g è y f y m l e è y y
d â s f e a l m b l r b r h e h e i c x
g l a à a e a e v e e c i r l a s r r u
a t f b          q w a i d g v o v ê v c v
d ê x c          e a v a p é c n c c p n c
l a ç a          a v z x v r ô d' o n u d n
                 j t k a d e d i o v f
                 a c o t e a e r r g g
                 u e k u k b d z k
                 s u f y w e x d w
                 d r b h v o p i c
                 z h d y q a k a
                       a w e l
                       f s à
                       a g m
```

lampe

horloge

réfrigérateur

8 août

oreiller

frère

pomme

cousine

lit

melon d'eau

ISBN: 978-1-927042-16-8

1 Les objets de classe
School Supplies

A. 1. m
   2. m
   3. f
   4. A: m
      B: f
      C: f
      D: m
      E: m
      F: f
   5. un tableau blanc : m
      un sac à dos : m
      une règle : f
      un cartable : m

B. 1. le livre   2. le pupitre
   3. le bureau   4. la chaise
   5. le tableau noir 6. le tapis

C. tapis ; stylo ; gomme ; cartable ;
   chaise ; marqueur ; sac à dos ; cahier ;
   règle ; papier

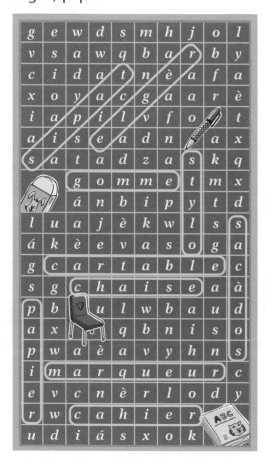

D. les crayons ; les livres ; les pupitres ;
   des bureaux ; des règles ; des tableaux ;
   les chaises ; des stylos

E. 1a. cartable   b. cartables
   2a. C'est une gomme.
    b. Ce sont des gommes.
   3a. C'est une règle.
    b. Ce sont des règles.
   4a. C'est une chaise.
    b. Ce sont des chaises.

2 À l'école
At School

B. le concierge
   l'étudiant
   le professeur
   la secrétaire
   la directrice
   1. la directrice
   2. la secrétaire
   3. l'étudiant
   4. le professeur
   5. le concierge

C. 1. C ; la cafétéria
   2. A ; la cour d'école
   3. B ; la salle de classe

D. 1. la classe de musique
   2. la bibliothèque
   3. Est-ce que je peux aller à la salle de
      classe?

3 La famille
Family

B. grand-père ; mère ; grand-mère ; père ;
   fille ; frère ; fils ; bébé ; animal domestique ;
   sœur

C. (Individual answer)

D. fils

Voici ; grand-père

Voici ; mère

Voici ; cousine

Voici ; fille

Voici ; l'oncle

Voici ; père

famille

E. 1. la mère   2. la grand-mère

3. la sœur   4. Jean ; de

5. le cousin

4 Les jours de la semaine
The Days of the Week

B. 4 jeudi ; 1 lundi ; 7 dimanche ; 6 samedi ;
3 mercredi ; 2 mardi ; 5 vendredi

C. les jours de la semaine

lundi

mardi

mercredi

jeudi

vendredi

samedi

dimanche

le calendrier

un jour

D. les jours de la semaine

lundi

mardi

mercredi

jeudi

vendredi

la fin de semaine

samedi

dimanche

E. 1. jeudi   2. samedi

3. vendredi   4. calendrier

5. la fin de semaine

F. 1. lundi ; je vais à

2. mardi ; je vais à

3. mercredi ; je vais à

4. jeudi ; je vais à

5. vendredi ; je vais à

6. samedi ; je vais à

7. dimanche ; je vais à

5 Les mois de l'année
The Months of the Year

B. (Individual answer)

C. 1. août   2. mai

3. janvier   4. octobre

D. janvier

février

mars

avril

mai

juin

juillet

août

septembre

octobre

novembre

décembre

E.

janvier

février

mars

avril

mai

juin

juillet

août

septembre

octobre

novembre

décembre

F. 1. A: dimanche 29 décembre

  B: Aujourd'hui c'est le mardi 19 février 2013.

  C: Aujourd'hui c'est le lundi 26 août 2013.

  2. (Individual answer)

6 Les nombres : de 1 à 15
Numbers: 1 to 15

B.

C. 1. cinq ; treize

  2. huit

  3. onze

  4. trois

  5. douze

D. A: douze crayons

  B: huit stylos

  C: dix cahiers

  D: quatre chaises

  E: quatorze paires de ciseaux

E. cinq pommes ; douze fraises ; Coupez quatre bananes ; Ajoutez quinze grains de raisin ; Coupez un melon d'eau ; huit ; d'orange

F. 1. Il y a   2. Il y a quatre

  3. Il y a quatorze 4. Il y a cinq

  5. Il y a dix

7 L'heure et le temps du jour
The Hour and the Time of Day

B. 1. 9 h 15   2. 11 h

  3. 4 h 30   4. 9 h 45

  5. 2 h 44   6. 7 h 30

  7. 8 h   8. 12 h 26

C. 1. 4 h 25   2. 18 h 37

  3. 17 h 11   4. 7 h 03

  5. 22 h 20   6. 14 h 30

  7. 1 h 05   8. 13 h 45

D. le matin ; l'après-midi ; le soir

  1. le soir   2. le matin

  3. l'après-midi   4. le soir

  5. l'après-midi   6. le soir

  7. le matin

E. 1. 8 h 10 ; le matin

  2. 20 h 14 ; le soir

  3. 16 h ; l'après-midi

F. A: Paris ; Il est 14 h 45.

  B: Quelle heure est-il à Toronto? ; Il est 10 h 30.

  C: Quelle heure est-il à Londres? ; Il est 20 h 35.

8 Les pronoms personnels sujets
Personal Subject Pronouns

B. 1. elle ; il   2. elle

  3. elle   4. il

  5. il   6. elle

  7. il   8. elle

  9. il   10. elle

C. 1. ils   2. ils
   3. elles   4. elles
   5. ils   6. ils
   7. ils

D. 1. a   2. avons
   3. ont   4. avez
   5. as   6. ont
   7. ai

E. (Suggested answers)

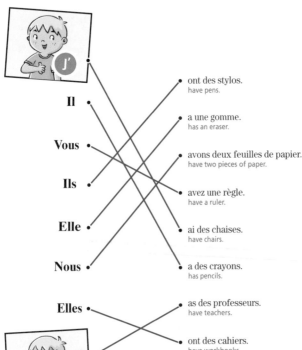

Il •   • ont des stylos.
                      have pens.

                    • a une gomme.
Vous •   has an eraser.

                    • avons deux feuilles de papier.
Ils •   have two pieces of paper.

                    • avez une règle.
Elle •   have a ruler.

                    • ai des chaises.
Nous •   have chairs.

                    • a des crayons.
                      has pencils.

Elles •   • as des professeurs.
                      have teachers.

                    • ont des cahiers.
                      have workbooks.

F. 1. Ils   2. Il
   3. Elles   4. Il
   5. Il   6. Ils

9 Chez moi
At My House

B. 1. une table ; une chaise
   2. une lampe ; un canapé
   3. un oreiller ; un lit

C. 1. est
   2. êtes
   3. sont
   4. suis
   5. es ; es

D. 1. bain
   2. Elle est dans la salle à manger.
   3. Il est dans le salon.
   4. Il est dans la cuisine.
   5. Il est dans la chambre à coucher.
   6. Elle est dans la buanderie.

E. Où est le réfrigérateur? ;
   Où est la machine à laver?

F. 1. le toit
   2. A: Il est dans le salon.
      B: Elle est dans la salle de bain.
      C: Il est dans la chambre à coucher.

10 Les couleurs
Colours

B. 1. l'orange
   2. le vert foncé
   3. le rose
   4. le violet

C.

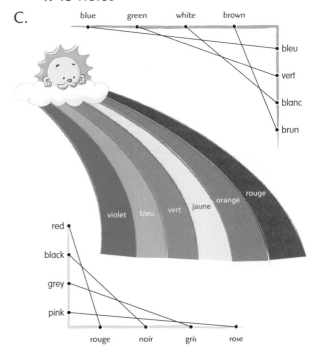

D. 1. le rouge   2. le bleu

3. le vert   4. l'orange

5. le jaune   6. le noir

7. le rose

E. A: avez ; bleues

B: Marie a un sac à dos violet.

C: Nous avons des cartables orange.

D: Il a une gomme verte.

F. J'aime l'orange.

J'aime le jaune.

J'aime le bleu.

J'aime le violet.

Je n'aime pas le vert.

Je n'aime pas le rouge.

Je n'aime pas le noir.

Je n'aime pas le brun.

I: la fenêtre

J: la lampe

C. Simon: E

You...: G

I like...: A

Where is...?: I

We are...: F

It is in...: B

They are...: H

What time is it?: C

It is 4 p.m.: D

D. 1. B   2. A

3. C   4. A

5. A   6. C

7. A   8. B

La révision
Revision

A. 1. un livre

2. une paire de ciseaux

3. des sœurs

4. une toilette

5. la salle à manger

6. le brun

7. ils

8. jeudi

9. 4 h 40

10. la bibliothèque

11. une machine à laver

12. cinq

B. A: le matin

B: la grand-mère

C: quatre

D: décembre

E: sept marqueurs

F: le bébé

G: le crayon

H: le canapé

Mots croisés
Crossword Puzzle

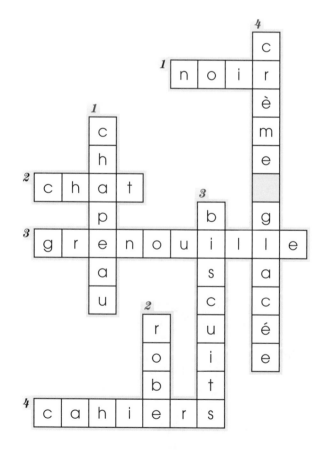

Mots cachés
Word Search

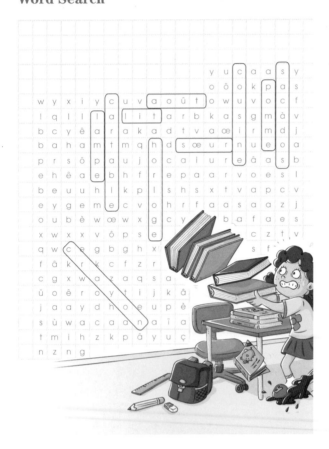

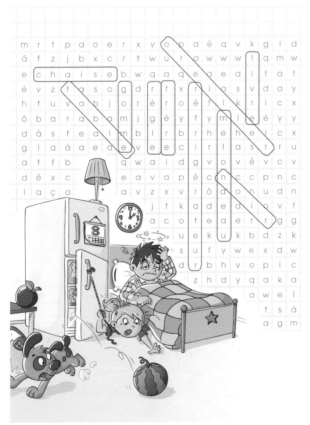